Quick Start Guides

# The Essential
# VEGAN
# COOKBOOK

A Quick Start Guide

To

Vegan Cooking

## Easy Plant-Based Recipes For Every Day.
## Quick And Delicious Healthy Vegan Recipes

First published in 2019 by Erin Rose Publishing

Text and illustration copyright © 2019 Erin Rose Publishing

Design: Julie Anson

ISBN: 978-1-9161523-4-2

A CIP record for this book is available from the British Library.

DISCLAIMER: This book is for informational purposes only and not intended as a substitute for the medical advice, diagnosis or treatment of a physician or qualified healthcare provider. The reader should consult a physician before undertaking a new health care regime and in all matters relating to his/her health, and particularly with respect to any symptoms that may require diagnosis or medical attention.

While every care has been taken in compiling the recipes for this book we cannot accept responsibility for any problems which arise as a result of preparing one of the recipes. The author and publisher disclaim responsibility for any adverse effects that may arise from the use or application of the recipes in this book. Some of the recipes in this book include nuts or other allergens. If you have an allergy it's important to avoid these.

# CONTENTS

## Vegan Recipes

# INTRODUCTION

Whether you are just beginning a plant-based vegan diet, doing Veganuary, detoxing, boosting your energy or expanding your range of vegan recipes, this book has something for you. The Essential Vegan Recipe Book For Beginners provides you with wholesome, nutritious plant-based recipes to make vegan cooking simple and delicious!

You can get start your vegan diet straight away as this comprehensive book makes cooking vegan meals fast and easy. When beginning a plant-based vegan diet, the first step is to understand what you can and can't eat and to prepare your cupboards with alternatives and substitutions for when hunger strikes. A plant-based diet will provide you with abundant minerals, vitamins, micro-nutrients and antioxidants and your taste buds will relish the variety of flavours and textures.

Even if you give it a go for a month, you will be surprised how easy it is and how great you feel. 'Veganuary' (going vegan for January) has been a catalyst for many to make veganism a more permanent diet and year round lifestyle improvement. Veganism is not just a trend. It is a lifestyle and it's here to stay! During the 2018 Veganuary campaign, an estimated 150,000 people worldwide took part and switched to a sustainable plant-based diet. Veganism is increasing at such a fast rate as more and more people feel the benefits.

The recipes in the vegan cookbook are full of wholefoods and fresh ingredients which are easily sourced in most supermarkets. They contain nutritious ingredients which go naturally together, improving digestion, reducing bloating and removing any need for food combining to prevent animal protein and carbohydrates being eaten together.

If you are ready to try some delicious plant-based vegan recipes, read on!

# Starting A Vegan Diet

Going vegan out of concern for animals is the number one reason people begin a plant-based diet. By following a vegan diet you are making a decision to take steps to prevent harm, cruelty and suffering to animals. For some, a vegan lifestyle is taken even further and includes avoiding products which contain ingredients derived from animals, such as clothing, cosmetics, cleaning products and clothing which are not vegan.

Another benefit of eating a plant-based diet is that it can save you money on your grocery bills as vegan forms of protein tend to be less expensive.

A large portion of plant based food often contains fewer calories than a meal which includes meat, so healthy weight loss is a bonus. You are likely to exceed your '5 a day' fruit and vegetable intake, and you will be loading up on nutrient dense whole foods.

Hormones, chemicals and preservatives in meat, especially the processed variety, are linked with chronic illnesses so you'll be avoiding these. A plant-based vegan diet is high in nutrients and natural fibre. You can tuck into healthy protein sources, like legumes, grains, nuts and seeds which are a source of amino acids, necessary to maintain good health. Iron is available in broccoli, green leafy vegetables, grains and dried fruit like raisins and apricots. There have been concerns that a vegan diet may not provide enough vitamin B12 and omega 3 oils, so if you are concerned you can safeguard your intake with a good quality supplement.

The meat industry is the third largest contributor to climate change. Raising livestock for food involves transportation which produces emissions which have a negative impact on the environment. The farming of vast numbers of cattle requires vast fuel resources, water and land which is used for animal feed crops. So much of the meat in our supply is wasted and a reduction in meat production can help reduce greenhouse gas.

# What Can I Eat?

## Foods To Avoid

### Avoid all animal products including the following:

- Beef
- Chicken
- Pork
- Turkey
- Lamb
- Fowl
- Fish
- Venison
- Veal
- Animal Fat

- Eggs
- Milk
- Cream
- Cheese
- Yogurt
- Crème Fraîche
- Fromage Frais
- Butter
- Honey
- Gelatine

## Foods You Can Eat

**Fruits & Vegetables**

- Avocados
- Aubergine (Eggplant)
- Broccoli
- Beetroot
- Brussels Sprouts
- Cauliflower
- Capers
- Cabbage
- Celeriac
- Celery
- Courgette (Zucchini)
- Cucumber
- Carrots
- Garlic
- Kale
- Lettuce
- Fennel
- Mushrooms
- Onions
- Marrow
- Peppers

- Parsnip
- Peas
- Potatoes
- Radishes
- Rocket (Arugula)
- Seaweeds like nori and dulse
- Spring Onions (Scallions)
- Shallots
- Soya
- Spinach
- Sweet Potatoes
- Swede
- Tomatoes
- Turnip
- Apples
- Bananas
- Blackberries
- Blueberries
- Grapefruit
- Kiwi Fruit
- Lemons
- Limes

- Mango
- Oranges
- Pineapple
- Raspberries
- Redcurrants
- Lychees
- Peaches
- Pears
- Persimmon
- Nectarines
- Strawberries

## Dried fruit

- Raisins
- Cranberries
- Currants
- Dates
- Bananas
- Apples
- Figs
- Sultanas
- Apricots
- Prunes

## Herbs & Spices

- Parsley
- Basil
- Bay Leaves
- Oregano
- Thyme
- Chives
- Cardamom Seeds
- Coriander (Cilantro)
- Lemon Balm
- Tarragon
- Dill
- Sage
- Cumin
- Turmeric
- Cayenne Pepper
- Mustard
- Ginger
- Chilli
- Nutmeg
- Allspice
- Star Anise
- Cinnamon
- Paprika
- Asafoetida

## Pulses, Nuts & Seeds

- Brazil Nuts
- Almonds
- Coconuts
- Walnuts
- Pecans
- Pine Nuts
- Pistachios
- Hazelnuts
- Peanuts
- Cashew Nuts
- Soybeans (Edamame)
- Black Beans
- Kidney Beans
- Cannellini Beans
- Haricot Beans
- Kidney Beans
- Chickpeas (Garbanzo Beans)
- Aduki Beans
- Pinto Beans
- Lentils
- Peas
- Chia Seeds
- Pumpkin Seeds
- Hemp Seeds
- Flaxseeds (Linseeds)
- Poppy Seeds
- Sesame Seeds
- Sunflower Seeds
- All nut butters, nut milks and nut oils.

## Grains & Cereals

- Rice
- Quinoa
- Buckwheat
- Oats
- Corn
- Amaranth
- Polenta
- Millet
- Wheat
- Barley
- Rye
- Bulgur Wheat
- Couscous

## Soya Products

- Tofu
- Soya Milk

- Soya Yogurt
- Soya Cheese
- Soya Protein
- Tempeh
- Miso

**Additional**

- Dairy-Free Dark Chocolate, Cacao Nibs or 100% Cocoa Powder
- Agave Nectar
- Maple Syrup
- Blackstrap Molasses
- Golden Syrup
- Sugar
- Tahini
- Nut Butters: like peanut butter, cashew butter and almond butter
- Nutritional Yeast
- Olive Oil
- Coconut Oil
- Vanilla Extract, Vanilla Pods
- Vinegar
- Soy Sauce
- Tabasco Sauce
- Coconut Cream/Coconut Milk

Always check with your medical advisor or doctor before embarking on any radical dietary changes, especially if you suffer from any medical condition, to ensure that it is safe and appropriate for you to do so.

# The Essential Vegan Substitutes

If you are new to vegan cooking it may take a little getting used to and you may wish to experiment to find your favourite ingredients. Due to demand, there are now more vegan foodstuffs on offer at the supermarket, ranging from vegan cheese, to soya cream and cashew milk. In terms of desired flavour and texture, these may be an acquired taste, but they will expand your meal variety.

Finding a plant-based milk is probably the most important. Almond milk is one of the most popular. It does not have a particularly strong flavour and is a good 'milky' consistency without being too thin. Soya milk is still popular and like almond milk is available sweetened or unsweetened. The range of plant milks available is still expanding. Once you have found plant-based milks you like, you can stock up as they keep well.

As an egg replacement in recipes which require binding, you can use chickpea flour (garbanzo bean flour/gram flour), or ground flaxseeds (linseeds). You could also use scrambled tofu as a substitute for scrambled egg.

Vegetable bouillon is a suitable replacement for meat stocks and this is another great store cupboard food.

Try coconut yogurt or soya yogurt as an alternative to dairy yogurt. Coconut yogurt is particularly delicious although it usually isn't cheap. These are available in the chilled section at the supermarket.

There are many solutions to not having butter. You can use peanut butter, cashew butter, almond butter, olive oil, coconut oil and mixed seed butter (this is so good!). Another possibility is margarine although you will need to check the labelling to make sure it is vegan. The drawback with margarines is that they can contain unhealthy hydrogenated fats.

Maple syrup, molasses, brown rice syrup and agave nectar can be used in place of honey. Dates can be added to recipes and give a delicious toffee flavour plus they contain fibre which slows down the sugar absorption.

Try not to over indulge on sweet things as too much sugar is never a good thing and can leave you with cravings. Some people choose to avoid cane sugar as some brands use animal bone char in the refining process.

Good quality chocolate is good for you and you don't have to give it up. There are dairy-free chocolates available plus 100% cocoa powder and cacao nibs.

Tofu is a nutritious protein which can be added to many dishes. It can be kept in the fridge or freezer in various forms like mince, blocks of smoked tofu and silken tofu for desserts. Again, you may need to experiment to find one you like.

Avoiding eating meat may be the greatest challenge for some. There are plenty of ready-made alternatives on the market including bacon, cheese, burgers, meat and meat balls which are all suitable for vegans. However, to avoid too many additives in your food, home-cooked meals are still better.

# Reading the Labels

If you wish to be sure a product is vegan it is worth checking the labels. Even products which appear to be free from animal products can contain non-vegan ingredients, often in the form of a dairy product. Some products carry the 'suitable for vegans' logo, however this is not currently on all products. Check the labels to find out whether a product is really vegan. Some of these are obvious and others less so. It is also worth checking that your plant milk does not have whey added to it!

- Animal Fats
- Beef Extract
- Beef Stock
- Beeswax
- Butter Fat
- Butter Oil
- Butter Ester
- Butter Milk
- Bone Char
- Bone Phosphate
- Carmine
- Casein
- Casein Hydrolysate
- Caseinates
- Curds
- Ghee

- Gelling Agent
- Lactose
- Lactalbumin
- Lactoferrin
- Lactose
- Lactulose
- Lactitol
- L-Cysteine
- Milk Protein Hydrolysate
- Whey
- Whey Protein Hydrolysate
- Albumen
- Dried Egg
- Egg Solids
- Mayonnaise
- Modified Milk

- Meringue
- Cochineal
- Aspic
- Tallow
- Collagen
- Elastin
- Cod Liver Oil
- Fish Oil
- Gelatine
- Rennet
- Pepsin
- Shellac

**E numbers which are derived from animal products are;**

- E901
- E120
- E966
- E441
- E542
- E904
- E910
- E920
- E921

# Vegan Recipes

# VEGAN BREAKFASTS

# Chocolate & Avocado Smoothie

## Ingredients

100mls (3½ fl oz) almond milk

1 banana, peeled

1 apple, peeled and cored

½ avocado, stone removed and peeled

1 tablespoon cacao nibs or vegan cocoa powder

Squeeze of lemon juice

SERVES 1

## Method

Toss all of the ingredients into a food processor and blitz until smooth and creamy. Drink straight away.

# Creamy Mango Smoothie

## Ingredients

1 mango, peeled and stone removed

1 avocado, peeled and stone removed

1 apple, cored

1 tablespoon flaxseeds (linseeds)

Juice of ½ lime

SERVES 1

## Method

Put all the ingredients into a blender with just enough water to cover the ingredients. Blitz until smooth and creamy.

# Grapefruit & Carrot Zinger

## Ingredients

1 large carrot, peeled and chopped
1 apple, cored and chopped
1 pink grapefruit, peeled

SERVES
1

## Method

Place all of the ingredients into a blender with just enough water to cover them and blitz until smooth.

# Coconut, Lime & Ginger Juice

## Ingredients

200mls (7fl oz) coconut water

Juice of ½ of a lime

1cm (½ inch) chunk of fresh ginger, peeled and finely crushed

SERVES
1

## Method

Mix all of the ingredients in a glass and add a few ice cubes. Drink straight away. This makes a lovely refreshing drink which keeps hunger away.

# Strawberry Protein Smoothie

## Ingredients

50g (2oz) frozen blueberries

50g (2oz) frozen strawberries

150mls (5fl oz) soya milk

1 scoop vegan protein powder

SERVES
1

## Method

Place all of the ingredients into a blender and blitz until smooth.

# Chocolate & Banana Protein Smoothie

## Ingredients

1 banana

1 tablespoon 100% vegan cocoa powder or cacao nibs

1 teaspoon chia seeds

1 scoop vegan protein powder

100mls (3½ fl oz) almond milk

SERVES
1

## Method

Place all the ingredients into a food processor and mix until smooth and creamy.

# Lush Green Smoothie

## Ingredients

50g (2oz) spinach
1 pear, core removed
1/2 of a cucumber
Flesh of 1 avocado
Squeeze of lemon juice

**SERVES 1**

## Method

Place all of the ingredients into a blender and add just enough water to cover them. Blitz until smooth and creamy. Serve and drink immediately.

# Raspberry & Coconut Overnight Oats

## Ingredients

100g (3½ oz) coconut yogurt or coconut milk
100g (3½ oz) raspberries
50g (2oz) oats
1 tablespoon desiccated (shredded) coconut

100mls (3½ fl oz) almond or soya milk
1 tablespoon chopped almonds

**SERVES 1**

## Method

Place the oats, coconut and almonds into a bowl. Pour in the almond milk and coconut milk and stir well. Sprinkle the raspberries on top. Cover it and store it in the fridge until ready to eat.

# Berry Smoothie Bowl

## Ingredients

150g (5oz) mixed berries; raspberries, strawberries, blueberries, redcurrants

150mls (5fl oz) soya or almond milk

1 banana, peeled and chopped

1 teaspoon chia seeds

1 scoop vegan protein powder

Extra berries for topping

## Method

Place the berries and soya/almond milk into a blender and process until smooth and creamy. Pour it into a bowl. Place the chopped banana, berries, chia seeds on top, in lines or sections to suit. Eat straight away. You can also add different toppings, like oats, granola, chopped nuts, vegan chocolate, coconut, coconut yogurt or seeds.

# Savoury Protein Pancakes

## Ingredients

100g (3½ oz) chickpea flour (garbanzo flour/gram flour)

½ teaspoon baking powder

½ teaspoon garlic powder

½ teaspoon turmeric

100mls (3½ fl oz) water plus 2 extra tablespoons water

1-2 tablespoons olive oil

Pinch of salt

**SERVES 2**

## Method

In a bowl, mix together the chickpea flour (garbanzo flour/gram flour) baking powder, garlic powder, turmeric and salt. Slowly whisk in the water until you have a smooth batter. Heat the oil in a frying pan. Pour in half of the mixture and cook until golden, then turn it over and cook on the other side. Repeat for the remaining mixture.

You can serve the pancakes with a wide variety of fillings like avocado, tahini, mushrooms, tomatoes, radish, herbs, hummus, spinach, peppers, onions, cucumber, olives and legumes.

# Banana French Toast & Maple Syrup

## Ingredients

- 4 slices of thick bread
- 2 bananas, peeled and chopped
- 2 tablespoons chickpea flour (garbanzo bean flour/gram flour)
- 2 tablespoon ground almonds (almond meal/almond flour)
- 2 teaspoons ground cinnamon
- 200mls (7fl oz) almond milk or other plant based milk
- 2 tablespoons maple syrup
- 1 teaspoon vanilla extract
- 1 tablespoon olive oil

**SERVES 4**

## Method

Place the flour, ground almonds (almond meal/almond flour), cinnamon, almond milk and vanilla extract into a bowl and whisk them together. Heat the olive oil in a frying pan. Dip the bread in the batter mixture and coat it completely. Gently place the bread into the frying pan and cook until slightly golden. Turn it over and cook on the other size. Serve some banana slices on top and spoon some maple syrup over the top. Enjoy.

# Chocolate & Nut Banana Yogurt

**SERVES 1**

## Ingredients

100g (3½ oz) coconut yogurt

1 banana, peeled and mashed

1-2 tablespoons chopped hazelnuts

1-2 teaspoons cacao nibs or 100% cocoa powder

## Method

Stir the banana into the coconut yogurt and mix well. Place half of the mixture into a serving bowl or glass and sprinkle on half of the hazelnuts and cacao nibs/ cocoa powder on top. Spoon the remaining yogurt mixture on top and add the remaining nuts and chocolate.

# Apple & Cinnamon Porridge

## Ingredients

200g (7oz) oats

1 tablespoon ground almonds (almond meal/almond flour)

2 large apples, cored, peeled and chopped

1 teaspoon ground cinnamon

450mls (15fl oz) almond milk

**SERVES 2**

## Method

Place the apples and cinnamon into a saucepan with a little water and cook them on a low heat until the apples have completely softened. Set them aside. Place the oats, almonds and plant milk into a saucepan and cook them on a medium heat, stirring well, until they porridge has thickened. Serve the porridge into bowls and spoon the apple mixture on top. You can add an extra sprinkling of cinnamon if you like.

# VEGAN LUNCHES

# Tomato & Basil Soup

## Ingredients

450g (14oz) tinned chopped tomatoes

1 onion, peeled and chopped

1 large handful fresh basil, chopped

450mls (1 pint) vegetable stock (broth)

2 teaspoons balsamic vinegar

1 tablespoon olive oil

Sea salt

Freshly ground black pepper

SERVES
2

## Method

Heat the olive oil in a saucepan. Add the onion and cook until it has softened. Pour in the tomatoes, stock (broth) and balsamic vinegar and bring them to the boil. Reduce the heat and simmer for around 10 minutes. Stir in half of the fresh basil and season with salt and pepper. Using a hand blender or food processor, blitz the soup to a smooth consistency. Serve with a sprinkling of fresh basil.

# Green Pea Soup

## Ingredients

200g (7oz) frozen peas

200g (7oz) frozen soya beans (edamame beans)

25g (1oz) rocket (arugula) leaves

6 spring onions (scallions), trimmed and chopped

A handful of fresh parsley, chopped

450mls (15fl oz) hot vegetable stock (broth)

300mls (½ pint) almond milk or soya milk

**SERVES 4**

## Method

Put the soya beans, peas, vegetable stock (broth) and spring onions (scallions) into a saucepan. Bring it to the boil and simmer for five minutes. Add the parsley and rocket (arugula) leaves and almond/soya milk. Pour only half of the soup mixture into a food processor and process until smooth. Return the blended soup to the saucepan and stir with the chunky soup to attain a creamy wholesome texture. Serve and enjoy.

# Sweetcorn Chowder

## Ingredients

300g (11oz) sweetcorn

2 stalks of celery, finely chopped

1 onion, peeled and chopped

1 red pepper (bell pepper), finely sliced

1/4 teaspoon chilli flakes

1/2 teaspoon paprika

1/2 teaspoon Cajun spice

1 large handful fresh coriander (cilantro) leaves, chopped

900mls (1 1/2 pints) warm vegetable stock (broth)

400mls (14fl oz) coconut milk

1 tablespoon olive oil

**SERVES 4**

## Method

Heat the oil in a large saucepan, add in the onion, celery and pepper and cook for 5 minutes. Add the sweetcorn, vegetable stock (broth), coconut milk, chilli flakes, Cajun spice and paprika bring it to the boil. Reduce the heat and simmer for 15 minutes. Using a hand blender or food processor, whizz the soup until only partially blended to a chunky texture. Sprinkle in the coriander (cilantro) and stir. Serve and enjoy.

# Chunky Chilli Bean Soup

## Ingredients

400g (14oz) tin kidney beans, drained and rinsed

3 large carrots, peeled and chopped

1 onion, peeled and finely chopped

3 cloves of garlic, chopped

1 teaspoon chilli powder

1 red pepper (bell pepper)

1 yellow pepper, deseeded and chopped

600mls (1 pint) hot vegetable stock (broth)

2 teaspoons paprika

1 tablespoon olive oil

Salt and freshly ground black pepper

**SERVES 4**

## Method

Heat the oil in a large saucepan, add the onion, peppers, garlic and carrots and cook for 5 minutes, stirring occasionally. Add in the paprika, chilli powder and vegetable stock (broth) and bring to the boil. Add in the kidney beans and warm them through. Season with salt and pepper.

# Minestrone Soup

## Ingredients

- 400g (14oz) tin of cannellini beans, drained
- 400g (14oz) tin of chopped tomatoes
- 100g (3½ oz) cabbage, shredded
- 100g (3½ oz) dried spaghetti, snapped into pieces
- 2 stalks of celery, chopped
- 2 medium courgettes (zucchinis), chopped
- 2 cloves of garlic, chopped
- 2 carrots, peeled and finely chopped
- 1 medium potato, diced
- 1 large onion, peeled and chopped
- 1.4 litres (2½ pints) vegetable stock (broth)
- 1 tablespoons tomato purée (tomato paste)
- 2 tablespoons olive oil
- A small handful of fresh parsley, chopped

**SERVES 4**

## Method

Heat the olive oil in a large saucepan. Add the onion, carrots, celery and garlic and cook for 10 minutes, stirring occasionally. Add in the stock (broth), tomatoes and tomato purée (paste), bring to the boil, reduce the heat and simmer for 10 minutes. Add the potato, beans, potato, courgettes, cabbage and spaghetti and continue cooking for around 15 minutes or until the vegetables have softened. Serve with a sprinkling of fresh parsley.

# Tomato, Lentil & Smoked Paprika Soup

## Ingredients

SERVES
4

400g (14oz) tin chopped tomatoes
200g (7oz) red lentils
2 carrots, peeled and diced
1 onion, peeled and chopped
1.5 litres (2½ pints) hot vegetable stock (broth)
2 tablespoons chopped fresh parsley
2 teaspoons smoked paprika
1 tablespoon olive oil

## Method

Heat the oil in a saucepan. Add the onion and carrots and cook for 5 minutes. Add the lentils, tomatoes, paprika and stock (broth) and stir well. Bring it to the boil, cover and simmer for around 30 minutes or until the lentils are tender. Add in the parsley and stir well. Allow the soup to cool slightly, then using a hand blender or food processor blitz the soup is smooth. Serve into bowls.

# Buddha Bowls

## Ingredients

100g (3½ oz) cooked beans or lentils

75g (3oz) cooked (preferably roasted) chopped sweet potatoes

50g (2oz) red cabbage, finely chopped

1 packet of cooked wholegrain rice or quinoa

1 avocado, stone removed, peeled and sliced

1 tablespoon cashew nuts

1 teaspoon sesame seeds

½ teaspoon paprika

½ teaspoon chilli flakes

1 small handful of fresh coriander (cilantro)

FOR THE DRESSING:

1 tablespoon tahini

1 teaspoon lemon juice

1 tablespoon water

Pinch of cayenne pepper

Pinch of sea salt

# Method

Put the tahini, lemon juice, water, cayenne pepper and salt into a bowl and mix well. Add a little water or extra lemon juice if it seems too thick. Assemble your Buddha bowl starting at the bottom with the rice or quinoa. Add the sweet potatoes, avocado, cabbage, beans/lentils, nuts and seeds in individual piles on top. Sprinkle over the paprika, chilli and coriander (cilantro). Drizzle the dressing over the ingredients. Eat straight away.

The key to fast and tasty Buddha bowls is leftovers. Cook extra potatoes, vegetables and bean dishes to save time and energy preparing them from scratch, that way you can assemble a Buddha bowl straight from ingredients you already have in the fridge. The varieties you can make are endless. This recipe is for a basic Buddha bowl but you can include almost anything you like. You can use leftover roast vegetables, falafels, tofu, guacamole, couscous, hummus, sliced apple, grated carrots, celery, tomatoes, cauliflower, broccoli, spinach, sweetcorn and add a handful of nuts, seeds and fresh herbs. Add plenty of colours for vibrancy and great nutrition. Dressings will add even more variety and there are more recipes for these at the back.

# Avocado & Mixed Bean Salad

## Ingredients

- 400g (14oz) tin of pinto beans, drained and rinsed
- 400g (14oz) tin of cannellini beans, drained and rinsed
- 225g (8oz) sweetcorn, drained
- 8 spring onions (scallions), chopped
- 4 tomatoes, chopped
- 2 avocados, stone removed, peeled and sliced
- 1 little gem lettuce, washed and finely chopped
- 1 handful of fresh chives, chopped
- 1 handful of fresh coriander (cilantro) chopped
- 1 garlic clove, finely chopped
- 1 green pepper (bell pepper), chopped
- 1 red pepper (bell pepper), chopped
- 1 teaspoon paprika powder
- 1/2 teaspoon chilli powder (optional)
- 4 tablespoons olive oil or avocado oil
- Juice of 1 lemon

**SERVES 4**

## Method

Place the lemon juice, olive oil, paprika powder, garlic, salt and chilli in a bowl and mix well. In a large serving bowl, combine the beans, lettuce, sweetcorn, tomatoes, peppers (bell peppers), spring onions (scallions), chives and coriander (cilantro). Pour the oil mixture over the salad ingredients. Serve with slices of avocado on top.

# Chickpea, Lemon & Coriander Salad

## Ingredients

400g (14oz) tin of chickpeas (garbanzo beans), drained

200g (7oz) sweetcorn, drained

4 tablespoon fresh coriander (cilantro)

2 spring onions (scallions) finely chopped

1 tablespoon lemon juice

Sea salt

Freshly ground black pepper

**SERVES 2**

## Method

Place the chickpeas and sweetcorn into a bowl and add in the coriander (cilantro), spring onions (scallions) and lemon juice. Mix the ingredients well. Season with salt and pepper.

# VEGAN DINNERS

# Vegan Jambalaya

## Ingredients

400g (14oz) brown rice, uncooked

400g (14oz) tin of mixed beans

400g (14oz) tin of chopped tomatoes

4 cloves of garlic, chopped

2 stalks of celery, chopped

2 bay leaves

1 red pepper (bell pepper), deseeded and chopped

1 onion, peeled and chopped

1 teaspoon sea salt

1 teaspoon cayenne pepper

1 teaspoon dried basil

1 teaspoon dried oregano

1 teaspoon dried thyme

1 teaspoon sweet paprika

1/2 teaspoon smoked paprika

1 litre (1 1/2 pints) vegetable stock (broth)

1 tablespoon olive oil

1 tablespoons Tabasco sauce

2 tablespoons soy sauce

Small handful of fresh parsley, chopped

**SERVES 2**

## Method

Heat the oil in a large pan, add the onion and garlic and cook until softened. Add the red pepper (bell pepper), tomato and celery and cook until they begin to soften. Pour in the stock (broth), rice, Tabasco, soy sauce, herbs, bay leaves and spices. Stir well. Bring it to a boil then reduce the heat and simmer for around 35 minutes, stirring occasionally until the rice has absorbed the liquid and is completely cooked. Add the beans and warm them through. Season with salt. Remove the bay leaves. Sprinkle in the parsley then serve.

# Curried Chickpea Salad

## Ingredients

75g (3oz) unsalted cashew nuts

2 x 400g (14oz) tins of chickpeas (garbanzo beans), drained

2 tomatoes, chopped

2 large handfuls of lettuce leaves

6 spring onions (scallions), chopped

1 red pepper (bell pepper), chopped

2 tablespoons tahini

2 tablespoons lemon juice

2 tablespoons olive oil

1 tablespoon maple syrup

1 tablespoon water

1 teaspoon vinegar

1 tablespoon curry powder

1 small handful of fresh coriander (cilantro), chopped

**SERVES 4**

## Method

In a bowl, whisk together the tahini, lemon juice, olive oil, maple syrup, water, vinegar and curry powder. Place the chickpeas (garbanzo beans), tomatoes, onions and pepper into the bowl and toss them in the dressing mixture. Scatter the lettuce leaves onto plates and serve the mixture on top. Sprinkle on some cashew nuts and serve.

# Mexican Quinoa Casserole

## Ingredients

2 x 400g (2 x 14oz) tins of chopped tomatoes

400g (14oz) tin of black beans, drained and rinsed

175g (6oz) quinoa

150g (5oz) vegan cheese, chopped

150g (5oz) sweetcorn

3 cloves of garlic, finely chopped

1 tablespoon olive oil

1 onion, finely chopped

1 green pepper (bell pepper), deseeded and finely chopped

1 courgette (zucchini), diced

1 teaspoon paprika

1 teaspoon oregano

1 teaspoon chili powder

1/2 teaspoon ground cumin

Juice of 1/2 lime

400mls (14fl oz) vegetable stock (broth)

SERVES 6

## Method

Preheat the oven to 180C/360F. Cook the quinoa according to the instructions using the stock (broth) instead of water and then drain it. Place the onions, peppers, garlic, courgette (zucchini), beans, tomatoes and sweetcorn in a bowl and mix well. Add in the spices, oil and lime juice to the mixture. Scoop it into an ovenproof dish or roasting tin. Add in the quinoa and mix well. Transfer it to the oven and bake for 40 minutes. Remove the dish from the oven and scatter the vegan cheese on top. Return it to the oven and cook for another 5-10 minutes. Serve and eat straight away.

# Marinara 'Meatballs'

## Ingredients

**SERVES 2**

400g (14oz) tin of chickpeas

75g (3oz) tin of peas

2 cloves of garlic, chopped or ready-chopped garlic

1 jar of vegan ready-made tomato and basil sauce

1 red onion, peeled and chopped

1 red pepper (bell pepper), deseeded and roughly chopped

1 handful of spinach

1 teaspoon paprika

1 teaspoon onion powder

2 tablespoons gram flour (chickpea/garbanzo flour)

2 tablespoons olive oil

Sunflower oil for cooking

Extra gram flour for rolling

## Method

Heat the olive oil in a frying pan and add the onion, pepper and garlic and cook for 3 minutes. Transfer them to a food processor and add in the chickpeas (garbanzo beans), peas, spinach, paprika, onion powder, gram flour (chickpea flour/garbanzo bean flour) and olive oil. The mixture should be soft and slightly sticky, ready to roll into balls. If you need extra liquid try adding a little extra oil or a tablespoon or two of water. Take a spoonful of the mixture and roll it into a ball then coat it in a little gram flour. Cook the balls in hot oil in the frying pan until golden. Heat the tomato sauce. Serve the sauce with the meatballs. This goes well with pasta or spaghetti.

# Vegan Tagine

## Ingredients

2 x 400g (2 x 14oz) tins of chopped tomatoes

200g (7oz) red lentils

75g (3oz) dried apricots, chopped

25g (1oz) fresh root ginger, peeled and grated

3 parsnips, peeled and cut into small cubes

2 carrots, peeled and chopped

2 onions, peeled and cut into wedges

2 garlic cloves, finely chopped

2 tablespoons harissa paste

2 teaspoon ground coriander (cilantro)

2 teaspoon ground cumin

2 teaspoon ground cinnamon

1 butternut squash, peeled, deseed and cut into small cubes

1 litre (1½ pints) vegetable stock (broth)

1 tablespoon olive oil

A handful of fresh parsley, chopped

Sea salt

Freshly ground black pepper

**SERVES 4**

## Method

Heat the oil in a large lidded saucepan, add the onions, garlic and ginger and cook for around 5 minutes until they have softened. Add the coriander (cilantro), cumin and cinnamon and stir well. Add the harissa paste and stir well. Add in the parsnips, squash and carrots and cook for 5 minutes. Add the tomatoes, lentils, apricots and stock (broth) and bring it to the boil. Reduce the heat and simmer for 40 minutes. Remove the lid, season with salt and pepper and stir in the chopped parsley. Check that the vegetables are tender. Serve with couscous, rice or crusty bread.

# Cheesy Stuffed Peppers

## Ingredients

250g (9oz) rice

125g (4oz) mushrooms, chopped

100g (3½ oz) vegan cheese, chopped

50g (2oz) pine nuts

4 red peppers (bell peppers), deseeded and halved lengthways

4 spring onions (scallions), chopped

4 tomatoes, chopped

3 cloves of garlic, chopped

2 tablespoons olive oil

A small handful of fresh parsley

**SERVES 4**

## Method

Preheat the oven to 190C/380F. Cook the rice according to the instructions or alternatively use a pack of microwave rice. Heat the oil in a frying pan, add the spring onions, garlic, mushrooms and tomatoes and cook for around 5 minutes until they have softened. Add in the rice, vegan cheese, pine nuts and parsley and mix well. Place the peppers on a roasting in and spoon some of the stuffing mixture into each one. Transfer it to the oven and cook for around 20 minutes. Serve and eat straight away.

# Quick Chickpea Curry

## Ingredients

- 400g (14oz) tin of chickpeas (garbanzo beans)
- 400g (14oz) tin of chopped tomatoes
- 3 cloves of garlic, chopped
- 2cm (1 inch) chunk of fresh ginger, peeled and chopped
- 1 onion, peeled and chopped
- 1 teaspoon curry powder
- 1 teaspoon ground cumin
- 1 teaspoon ground coriander (cilantro)
- 1 teaspoon cayenne pepper
- 1 teaspoon ground turmeric
- 1 tablespoon olive oil
- Small handful of fresh coriander (cilantro)

**SERVES 4**

## Method

Heat the oil in a large pan, add the onions and cook until softened. Add the fresh ginger, garlic, cloves and spices and stir well. Add in the chickpeas (garbanzo beans) and tomatoes and heat them through. Sprinkle in the fresh coriander (cilantro). Serve with rice or warm naan bread.

# Curried Tofu & Roast Vegetables

## Ingredients

**FOR THE TOFU:**

1 block of tofu, cut into chunks

2.5cm (1 inch) chunk of fresh ginger root, finely chopped

1 clove of garlic, crushed

1 teaspoon chilli powder

1 teaspoon curry powder

1/2 teaspoon sea salt

1/2 teaspoon turmeric

1 tablespoon olive oil

Juice of 1 lemon

**FOR THE VEGETABLES:**

1 large aubergine (eggplant) cut into thick chunks

4 large tomatoes, de-seeded and cut into chunks

1 red pepper (bell pepper)

1 yellow pepper (bell pepper)

1 tablespoon olive oil

1 handful fresh coriander (cilantro), chopped

**SERVES 4**

## Method

For the tofu; place the chilli, salt, curry powder, turmeric, ginger, garlic, olive oil and lemon juice into a bowl and stir it well. Coat the tofu in the mixture. Place the vegetables into a large ovenproof dish and coat them in a tablespoon of olive oil. Scatter the tofu into the dish. Transfer the dish to the oven and cook at 180C/360F for around 35 to 40 minutes. Scatter the chopped coriander (cilantro) over the top and serve.

# Pesto Pepper & Tofu Kebabs

## Ingredients

250g (9oz) firm tofu, cubed

6 cherry tomatoes

3 tablespoons of Parmesan-free pesto

1 red pepper (bell pepper), deseed and cut into wide chunks

1 teaspoon salt

1 teaspoon white pepper

1/2 teaspoon onion powder

1 tablespoon olive oil

**SERVES 2**

## Method

Place the red pepper (bell pepper), pesto, salt, pepper, onion powder and olive oil into a bowl and mix well. Add the tofu and gently coat it in the mixture. Thread the tofu, pepper and tomatoes alternately onto metal skewers (if using bamboo skewers you will need to soak them in water first). Place the skewers under a hot preheated grill (broiler) and cook them for around 3 minutes on each side, turning them occasionally. Alternatively they can be cooked on a barbeque. Serve with rice, quinoa or salad.

# Lentil Dahl

## Ingredients

400g (14oz) jar passata or chopped tomatoes

400g (14oz) red lentils, rinsed

3 tablespoons vegan curry paste

2 cloves of garlic, minced

2cm (1 inch) chunk of fresh ginger, peeled and chopped

1 teaspoon ground turmeric

1 onion, peeled and chopped

1 teaspoon ground cumin

1 teaspoon chilli powder

1 teaspoon salt

1 tablespoon olive oil

SERVES 4

## Method

Place the lentils into a saucepan and cover them with water. Bring it to the boil and cook until the lentils are tender. You may need to add extra hot water during cooking. Heat the oil in a large pan, add the onion and cook until softened. In a small bowl, combine the curry paste, cumin, turmeric, chilli powder, salt, ginger and garlic. Stir the curry mixture into the onions and cook for 1 minute. Stir in the passata and bring it to a simmer. Add in the cooked lentils and mix well. Serve with rice.

# Cheese & Tomato Flatbread Pizza

**SERVES 2**

## Ingredients

6 sundried tomatoes, drained

2 slices vegan cheese, chopped

2 flatbreads

1 tablespoon tomato paste (purée)

1 tablespoon pine nuts

A few fresh basil leaves, chopped

Pinch of cayenne pepper

## Method

Preheat the oven to 200C/400F. Spread some tomato paste onto each flatbread. Sprinkle the pine nuts on top and add the tomatoes. Top if off with the vegan cheese pieces. Season with cayenne pepper. Lay the flatbread in a large roasting tin or baking sheet if you need more space. Transfer it to the oven and cook for 7-8 minutes. Sprinkle with basil before serving.

# Cajun Vegetable Skewers

## Ingredients

225g (8oz) mushrooms, halved

100g (3½ oz) cherry tomatoes

2 tablespoons Cajun spice mix

1 medium courgette (zucchini), sliced

1 red pepper (bell pepper), deseeded and cut into wide chunks

1 yellow pepper (bell pepper), deseeded and cut into wide chunks

1 onion, cut into 2cm (1 inch) pieces

2 tablespoons olive oil

**SERVES 4**

## Method

Place the oil and Cajun in a bowl and mix well. Add the vegetables to the bowl and stir until they are completely coated in the mix. Thread the vegetables alternately onto metal skewers (if you use bamboo skewers you will need to soak them in water first). Place the skewers under a hot pre-heated grill (broiler) and cook for around 3-4 minutes on each side.

# Speedy Bean Chilli

## Ingredients

- 2 x 250g (9oz) tinned of kidney beans or mixed beans, drained and rinsed
- 2 x 400g (14oz) tins of chopped tomatoes
- 2 mushrooms, finely chopped
- 1 large onion, peeled and chopped
- 3 teaspoons Cajun seasoning
- 2 teaspoon ground cumin
- 1 teaspoon paprika
- 1-2 teaspoons chilli powder
- 1 tablespoon olive oil
- Sea salt
- Freshly ground black pepper

**SERVES 4-6**

## Method

Heat the oil in a saucepan, add the onion and cook until softened. Add the mushrooms and cook for 2 minutes. Sprinkle in the Cajun seasoning, cumin, paprika and chilli powder and stir well. Add the beans and tomatoes to the saucepan. Bring it to the boil, reduce the heat and simmer for 20 minutes. Season with salt and pepper. Serve with rice or use the chilli as a filling for tacos with salad and a dollop of guacamole.

# Tofu & Coconut Curry

## Ingredients

- 400g (14oz) tofu
- 4 tomatoes, quartered
- 3 cloves of garlic, finely chopped
- 1 onion, finely chopped
- 1cm (½ inch) chunk of ginger, peeled and chopped
- 1 tablespoon curry powder
- 1 teaspoon garam masala
- 1 teaspoon ground cumin
- ¼ teaspoon turmeric
- 1 bay leaf
- 1 tablespoon chopped fresh coriander leaves
- 400mls (14fl oz) coconut milk
- 2 tablespoons lemon juice
- 1 tablespoons olive oil

**SERVES 4**

## Method

Drain the tofu and cut it into 1cm (½ inch) pieces. Heat the oil in a pan, add the onion, garlic, garam masala and ginger and cook for 5 minutes. Add the turmeric, curry, cumin and bay leaf and stir well. Pour in the coconut milk, tomatoes, lemon juice and turn off the heat. In a separate pan, heat a tablespoon of oil, add the tofu and cook until golden. Add the tofu pieces to the curry and stir well. Sprinkle in the coriander (cilantro) and serve.

# Tomato & Fennel Gratin

## Ingredients

2 x 400g (2 x 14oz) tinned chopped tomatoes
150g (5oz) vegan cheese, sliced
3 cloves of garlic, chopped
3 fennel bulbs, thinly sliced
1 onion, peeled and chopped
1 teaspoon dried mixed herbs
2 tablespoons olive oil

**SERVES 4**

## Method

Preheat the oven to 180C/360F. Scatter the fennel, garlic and onion into a roasting tin and drizzle in the oil. Toss the ingredients well. Transfer it to the oven and cook for 20 minutes. In a bowl, mix together the tomatoes with the dried mixed herbs. Pour the tomatoes into the roasting tin and return it to the oven for 40 minutes. Scatter the cheese over the bake and cook it in the oven for around 5 minutes. Serve with crusty bread.

# Smoked Tofu Satay

## Ingredients

225g (8oz) smoked tofu

2 tablespoons cornflour

1/4 teaspoon Chinese five-spice

300mls (10fl oz) vegetable oil for cooking

FOR THE SATAY SAUCE:

4 tablespoons smooth peanut butter

3 tablespoons rice wine vinegar

2 tablespoons toasted sesame

1 tablespoons soy sauce

1 tablespoon vegetable oil

1-2 teaspoons Tabasco sauce

1 teaspoon maple syrup

2 teaspoons fresh lime juice

**SERVES 2**

## Method

For the satay sauce, place all of the ingredients into a bowl and mix them well, or alternatively use a blender. Drain off any excess liquid from the tofu then cut it into 8 chunks. Put the cornflour and five-spice mix into a bowl and mix well. Coat the tofu in the spice mixture. Heat the oil in a wok over a high heat. Gently place each tofu chunk into the oil and cook for around 5 minutes or until they are crisp and golden. Remove the tofu from the wok using a slotted spoon. Once they are cool enough, thread the tofu chunks onto a skewer and serve with the satay sauce.

# Spanish Chickpea Casserole

## Ingredients

2 x 400 g tins of chopped tomatoes

250g (9oz) chickpeas (garbanzo beans)

200g (7oz) fresh spinach

3 cloves of garlic, chopped

3 teaspoons ground cumin

2 teaspoons smoked paprika

1 onion, peeled and chopped

1/4 teaspoon hot chilli powder

1/2 teaspoon salt

2 teaspoons brown sugar

1 tablespoon tomato purée (paste)

1 handful of fresh parsley, chopped

2 tablespoons olive oil

SERVES 4

## Method

Heat up the oil in a large frying pan, add the onion and cook for 5 minutes. Add the garlic and spices and stir well. Add in the tinned tomatoes, sugar and tomato purée. Bring it to a boil, reduce the heat and simmer for 10 minutes, stirring occasionally. Add in the chickpeas (garbanzo beans) and cook for 5 minutes. Add in the spinach and cook for around another 5 minutes until it has wilted. Serve with a sprinkling of parsley.

# Maple Roast Cauliflower

## Ingredients

8 parsnips, peeled and cut into lengthways
1 large cauliflower, sliced into florets, with the leaves
4 tablespoons olive oil
2 tablespoons maple syrup
A large handful of fresh parsley, chopped

**SERVES
4**

## Method

Preheat the oven to 180C/360F. Pour the olive oil and maple syrup into a large bowl. Add the cauliflower and parsnips and coat them in the mixture. Scatter the vegetables onto a roasting tin. Season with salt and pepper. Transfer them to the oven and cook for around 30 minutes or until the vegetables have softened. Sprinkle with parsley and serve.

# Falafels

## Ingredients

400g (14oz) panko breadcrumbs

3 cloves of garlic, peeled

2 x 400g (14oz) tins of chickpeas (garbanzo beans)

2 red chillies, chopped

2 teaspoons ground cumin

2 teaspoons ground coriander

½ teaspoon baking powder

½ teaspoon turmeric

1 small onion, chopped

1 small handful of fresh coriander (cilantro) chopped

1 small handful of fresh flatleaf parsley

Juice of 1 lime

SERVES 4

## Method

Place all of the ingredients into a food processor and mix until smooth. Using clean hands, take a small amount of the mixture and roll it into a small bite-size ball. Repeat for all the remaining mixture. You can either deep fry the falafels if you like them really crispy or cook them in hot oil in a frying griddle pan. Serve hot or cold. They are so versatile and can be added to salads, served with dips or as a filling for sandwiches and pitta bread.

# Pesto Baked Mushrooms

## Ingredients

8 large mushrooms
2 tablespoons vegan pesto
1 tablespoon olive oil

**SERVES 4**

## Method

Preheat the oven to 200C/400F. Lay the mushrooms on a baking tray and pour a little olive oil onto each one. Spoon some pesto sauce onto each one. Place them in the oven and cook for 8-10 minutes. Serve hot.

# Baked Apple Sprouts

## Ingredients

675g (1½ lbs) Brussels sprouts, trimmed and cut in half

4 sprigs of rosemary

3 apples, peeled, cored and sliced

3 tablespoons olive oil

A small handful of fresh parsley, chopped

**SERVES 4**

## Method

Preheat the oven to 200C/400F. Toss the sprouts, apple and oil together making sure everything is coated well with the oil. Add in the rosemary. Transfer it to the oven and cook for around 30 minutes or until the sprouts are tender. Sprinkle with parsley and serve.

# Biryani Vegetable Rice

## Ingredients

450g (1lb) basmati rice

150g (5oz) trimmed green beans, halved

3 tablespoons medium curry paste

1 medium cauliflower, broken into small florets

1 red pepper (bell pepper), deseeded and chopped

1 sweet potato, peeled and diced

1 onion, peeled and chopped

2 tablespoons olive oil

1 litre (1½ pints) vegetable stock (broth)

Juice of 1 lemon

A large handful coriander (cilantro) leaves, chopped

**SERVES 8**

## Method

Preheat the oven to 200C/400F. Toss the cauliflower, sweet potato and onion into a large roasting tin and coat them in the olive oil. In a bowl, mix together the stock (broth) and curry paste. Add the rice, pepper and green beans to the roasting tin. Pour the stock over the rice and mix well. Tightly cover the roasting tin with foil. Bake in the oven for 35 minutes then check if the rice is tender and the liquid has been absorbed. If necessary, continue cooking until the rice has softened. Add the lemon juice and some of the coriander (cilantro) into the rice and stir well. Scatter with the remaining coriander (cilantro). Serve and enjoy.

# Cannellini Bake

## Ingredients

**SERVES 4**

200g (7oz) vegan cheese, chopped

2 x 400g (2 x 14oz) tins of cannellini beans, rinsed and drained

2 x 400g (2 x 14oz) tins of chopped tomatoes

2 cloves of garlic, crushed

1 onion (chopped)

1 large handful of fresh basil, chopped

1 large handful of fresh parsley, chopped

1 teaspoon smoked paprika

1 tablespoon olive oil

## Method

Preheat the oven to 200C/400F. Pour the oil into an ovenproof dish and add in the onion, garlic, cannellini beans, tomatoes, basil and paprika. Season with salt and pepper. Transfer it to the oven and cook for 25 minutes. Remove the dish from the oven and scatter the vegan cheese over the top. Return it to the oven and cook for 10 minutes. Sprinkle with parsley and serve.

# Thai Mushroom & Vegetable Noodles

## Ingredients

- 450g (1lb) button mush-rooms, halved
- 200g (7oz) block of tofu, sliced
- 4 tablespoons vegan Thai red curry paste
- 4 spring onions (scallions), chopped
- 1 onion, peeled and chopped
- 1 pack of noodles
- 1 small handful of fresh coriander (cilantro)
- 1 teaspoon ground ginger
- 1/2 teaspoon Tabasco sauce
- 1 teaspoon maple syrup
- 1.4 litres vegetable stock (broth)
- 400mls (14oz) tin full-fat coconut milk
- 75mls (3fl oz) soy sauce
- 1 tablespoon olive oil
- Sprinkling of sesame seeds

**SERVES 4**

## Method

Heat the olive oil in a frying pan, add the onion, mushrooms, Tabasco, soy sauce, curry paste and ginger. Cook for 3 minutes. Pour in the stock (broth) and maple syrup and cook for 2 minutes. Pour in the coconut milk, reduce the heat and simmer for 10 minutes. In the meantime, place the tofu slices under a grill and cook until crisp, turning once during cooking. Cook the noodles according to the instructions. Serve the noodles into bowls and add some of the mushroom mixture into each one. Scatter on the sesame seeds, spring onions (scallions), coriander (cilantro) and tofu. Eat straight away.

# Vegetable Paella

## Ingredients

250 g (9oz) paella rice

125g (4oz) green beans, halved

125g (4oz) frozen broad beans

250g (9oz) marinated artichoke hearts, drained

2 cloves of garlic, crushed

1 onion, finely chopped

1 green pepper (bell pepper), deseeded and finely chopped

1 large handful of fresh parsley, chopped

1 teaspoon paprika

Large pinch of saffron

1 litre (1½ pints) hot vegetable stock (broth)

3 tablespoons olive oil

1 lemon, cut into wedges to garnish

**SERVES 4**

## Method

In a jug, stir the saffron into the vegetable stock (broth) and allow it to stand. Heat the olive oil in a large frying pan, add the onion and pepper and cook for 10 minutes. Add the garlic and stir well. Add the rice to the pan and coat it thoroughly in the oil. Add the paprika and green beans. Pour in the stock (broth) and stir well. Bring it to the boil, reduce the heat and simmer uncovered for 20 minutes. Add the artichokes and broad beans and stir well. Remove it from the heat, cover and let it stand for 5 minutes. Sprinkle with parsley. Serve with a wedge of lemon.

# Lentil Bake

## Ingredients

250g (9oz) lentils

50g (2oz) vegan cheese, chopped

1 carrot, peeled and finely chopped

1 onion, peeled and finely chopped

1 small handful of fresh parsley, chopped

1 small handful of fresh chives, chopped

450mls (15fl oz) vegetable stock (broth)

1 tablespoon olive oil

**SERVES 4**

## Method

Preheat the oven to 200C/400F. Pour the stock (broth) into a saucepan, add the lentils and cook for 12 minutes. Drizzle the olive oil into an ovenproof dish. Scatter the lentils into the dish and add the onion, carrot and herbs and mix well. Scatter the cheese over the top. Transfer it to the oven and cook for around 20 minutes. Serve and eat straight away.

# Pomegranate Couscous

## Ingredients

450mls (15fl oz) hot vegetable stock (broth)

450g (1lb) couscous

8 cherry tomatoes, chopped

2 teaspoons ground coriander (cilantro)

1 teaspoon ground cumin

1 teaspoon ground turmeric

1 teaspoon paprika

1 large handful parsley, chopped

1 pomegranate

1 cucumber, finely diced

4 tablespoons olive oil

**SERVES 4**

## Method

Place the couscous into a large bowl and pour the vegetable stock, (broth) over the top. Let it steep for 10 minutes and fluff the grains apart using a fork. In a bowl, combine the olive oil, cumin, turmeric and paprika. Pour the oil into the couscous and stir well. Add the tomatoes, cucumber and parsley to the bowl. Using the back of a spoon, firmly tap the pomegranate all over to loosen the seeds, then cut it in half and squeeze the seeds over the salad. Serve and enjoy.

# Pinto Bean & Avocado Tortilla Wraps

## Ingredients

100g (3½ oz) pinto beans

25g (1oz) sweetcorn

2 wholemeal tortilla wraps

¼ cucumber, peeled, deseeded and chopped

Flesh of 1 avocado

Juice ¼ lemon

1 teaspoon olive oil

**SERVES 1**

## Method

Place the avocado, olive oil and lemon juice in a food processor and mix until smooth and creamy. Put the sweetcorn, beans and cucumber into a bowl, drizzle the avocado mixture on top. Stir well. Lay the wraps out flat and spoon some of the mixture into the centre. Fold up the bottom and wrap the sides over the top. Serve and eat straight away.

# Roast Balsamic Peppers

## Ingredients

4 cloves garlic, chopped

2 red peppers (bell peppers), sliced

2 yellow pepper (bell peppers) sliced

1 green pepper (bell pepper), sliced

1 onion, chopped

1 teaspoon ground coriander (cilantro)

1 handful of fresh basil or marjoram, chopped

2 tablespoons balsamic vinegar

3 tablespoons olive oil

**SERVES 4**

## Method

Pour the olive oil into a roasting tin together with the balsamic vinegar and coriander (cilantro). Mix well. Add the peppers, onion and garlic and toss them in the oil. Transfer it to the oven and cook at 180C/360F for 25 minutes. Stir in the fresh herbs. Serve with fresh crusty bread and a green leafy salad.

# Vegan Shepherd's Pie

## Ingredients

- 400g (14oz) tin chopped tomatoes
- 400g (14oz) tin of brown lentils
- 900g (2lb) sweet potatoes, peeled and cut into chunks
- 50g (2oz) vegan cheese, chopped
- 2 onions, finely sliced
- 1 carrot, peeled and diced
- 1 tablespoon tomato puree
- 1 clove of garlic, crushed
- 1 teaspoon fresh thyme, chopped
- 1 teaspoon fresh rosemary, chopped
- 1 tablespoon olive oil
- 1 vegetable stock cube, crumbled
- 200mls (7fl oz) white wine
- 50mls (2fl oz) water

**SERVES 4**

## Method

Heat the oil in a frying pan, add the onion and cook for 5 minutes. Add the carrot, tomato purée (paste), garlic and herbs and cook for 2 minutes. Pour in the wine and simmer for 5 minutes. Add in the stock cube, tomatoes, lentils and water. Cook for 10 minutes, or until the carrots are tender. In the meantime, add the potatoes to a large saucepan, cover them with water and boil them until tender. Drain and mash the potatoes. Season with salt and pepper. Preheat the oven to 200C/400F. Scoop the lentil mixture into an ovenproof dish. Dollop the mash on top and spread it out. Scatter the cheese over the top. Transfer it to the oven and cook for around 30 minutes.

# Herby Roast Vegetables

## Ingredients

- 150g (5oz) cherry tomatoes, halved
- 150g (5oz) button mushrooms
- 3 celery stalks, chopped
- 3 cloves of garlic, peeled and chopped
- 2 carrots, peeled and roughly chopped
- 1 whole beetroot, washed and roughly chopped
- 1 large onion, chopped
- 1 courgette (zucchini), chopped
- 1 butternut squash, peeled and cut into chunks
- 1 teaspoon dried thyme
- 1 teaspoon dried oregano
- 1 large handful of fresh parsley
- 1 tablespoon olive oil
- Sea salt
- Freshly ground black pepper

**SERVES 4**

## Method

Place all of the vegetables into an ovenproof dish. Sprinkle in the dried herbs, garlic and olive oil and toss all of the ingredients together. Season with salt and pepper. Transfer them to an oven, preheated to 180C/360F and cook for 30-40 minutes or until all of the vegetables are softened. Scatter in the fresh parsley just before serving.

# Vegetable Fritters & Sweet Chilli Dip

## Ingredients

- 300g (11oz) cauliflower and/or broccoli florets
- 125g (4oz) gram flour (chickpea/garbanzo flour)
- 125mls (4fl oz) water
- 1/2 teaspoon ground coriander (cilantro)
- Sunflower oil for cooking
- Pinch of salt

FOR THE SWEET CHILLI DIP:

- 125g (4oz) sugar
- 3 cloves of garlic, finely chopped
- 3 tablespoons tomato ketchup
- 2 red chillies, finely chopped
- 2 tablespoons cornflour, mixed with 2 tablespoons water
- 1 teaspoon ground ginger
- 1/2 small red pepper (bell pepper), finely chopped
- 1/2 teaspoon salt
- 50mls (2fl oz) cider vinegar of rice wine vinegar
- 200mls (7fl oz) water

**SERVES 2**

## Method

For the sauce: Place the tomato ketchup, sugar, pepper, chillies, garlic, salt, ginger and chilli flakes into a saucepan and stir well. Pour in the water and vinegar and mix until smooth. Heat the sauce for around 10 minutes. Add just a little of the cornflour thickener at a time until it have your desired constancy. This recipe makes plenty, so you can store it ready to use. Once the mixture has cooled, transfer it to clean jars.

FOR THE FRITTERS: Place the flour, salt and ground coriander (cilantro) into a bowl and mix well. Add the water and whisk to a smooth batter. Heat the sunflower oil in a large frying pan. Coat the vegetables in the batter and cook it in the frying pan until golden. Turn it over and cook on the other side.

# Garlic & Tomato Sweet Potato Wedges

## Ingredients

SERVES 4

1 kg (2½ lb) sweet potatoes, washed and cut into wedges

6 large vine tomatoes, roughly chopped

4 cloves of garlic, finely chopped

2 onions, peeled and cut into wedges

2 tablespoons olive oil

Sea salt

Freshly ground black pepper

## Method

Preheat the oven to 200C/400F. Pour the olive oil into a roasting tin and add the garlic. Mix well. Add the sweet potato and toss it well in the garlic oil. Add in the tomatoes and onion and scatter them in one layer. You may need to use 2 roasting tins to do this. Transfer it to the oven and cook for around 40 minutes or until the wedges are tender. Season with salt and pepper.

# Mediterranean Quinoa

## Ingredients

250g (9oz) quinoa

4 mushrooms, chopped

3 cloves of garlic, peeled and finely chopped

2 large tomatoes, chopped

1 large courgettes (zucchinis), chopped

1 onion, peeled and finely chopped

1 green pepper (bell pepper), finely chopped

1 large handful fresh basil, chopped

1 small handful fresh chives, chopped

1 teaspoon dried mixed herbs

1 tablespoon olive oil

**SERVES 2**

## Method

Place the quinoa into a saucepan of hot water, bring it to the boil and simmer for 15 minutes. Drain off the excess water and fluff the quinoa with a fork. Transfer it to a large bowl. Heat the olive oil in a saucepan. Add in the onion, mushrooms and garlic and cook for 3 minutes. Add in the tomatoes, courgette (zucchini), green pepper (bell pepper) and dried mixed herbs. Cook until the vegetables have softened. Add the vegetables to the quinoa, add the fresh basil and chives and stir them through the quinoa. Serve and enjoy.

# Stuffed Butternut Squash

## Ingredients

- 200g (7oz) cherry tomatoes
- 100g (3½ oz) vegan cheese, chopped
- 50g (2oz) pine nuts
- 2 large butternut squash, halved and seeds removed
- 2 onions, peeled and quartered
- 2 cloves of garlic, chopped
- 1 courgette (zucchini), diced
- 1 red pepper (bell pepper), diced
- 1 tablespoon parsley
- 1 teaspoon thyme, chopped
- Pinch of cayenne pepper
- 3 tablespoons olive oil

**SERVES 4**

## Method

Preheat the oven to 200C/400F. Place the garlic, 2 tablespoons of oil, cayenne pepper and thyme into a bowl and mix well. Coat the butternut squash with the oil mixture. Lay the squash in a roasting tin, cut side up and transfer it to the oven. Cook for 35 minutes, or until the squash is tender. In the meantime, in a separate roasting tin, scatter the courgette (zucchini), red pepper (bell pepper), onion and drizzle a tablespoon of olive oil over the vegetables. Transfer it to the oven and cook for 20 minutes. Add the tomatoes and pine nuts to the vegetables and continue cooking for 10 minutes. Spoon some of the vegetable mixture into the squash. Sprinkle with cheese and parsley. Return it to the oven and continue cooking for 5-10 minutes or until the cheese has melted.

# Cashew Quinoa Salad & Maple Ginger Dressing

## Ingredients

FOR THE QUINOA:

300g (11oz) quinoa

200g (7oz) unsalted cashew nuts

150g (5oz) frozen peas

6 radishes, chopped

1 large carrot, peeled and grated (shredded)

1 bunch of spring onions (scallions), chopped

1 red pepper (bell pepper) chopped

1/2 cucumber, diced

FOR THE DRESSING:

3 tablespoons olive oil

2 tablespoons soy sauce

2cm (1 inch) piece of ginger root, grated (shredded)

1 teaspoon maple syrup

1/2 teaspoon chilli flakes

SERVES
4

## Method

Place the quinoa into a saucepan, cover it with hot water and cook for 15 minutes. Drain off the excess water and fluff the grains with a fork. Cook the peas in boiling water for 2-3 minutes or until heated through, then drain them. Mix the raw vegetables and cashew nuts in a large bowl and add in the quinoa. In separate bowl mix together the ingredients for the dressing then pour it into the salad. Stir well.

# Chinese Baked Tofu

## Ingredients

150g (5oz) regular tofu, sliced

2cm (1 inch) fresh root ginger, peeled and grated

1 clove of garlic, sliced

2 teaspoons soy sauce

Small handful of fresh coriander (cilantro)

Pinch of chilli flakes

**SERVES 4**

## Method

Preheat oven to 220C/400F. Place the tofu on a large piece of foil. Sprinkle it with garlic, ginger, soy sauce, coriander (cilantro) and chilli. Fold the foil over and seal the edges to make a parcel. Transfer it to the oven and cook for 15 minutes.

# Vegetable & Lemon Risotto

## Ingredients

- 100g (3½ oz) green beans, chopped
- 100g (3½ oz) risotto rice
- 50g (2oz) peas
- 1 carrot, finely grated
- 3 cloves of garlic, chopped
- 4 tablespoons nutritional yeast flakes (optional)
- 1 small onion, peeled and diced
- 1 small handful fresh parsley, chopped
- 1 teaspoon turmeric
- 600mls (1 pint) vegetable stock (broth)
- 1 tablespoon olive oil
- Juice of ½ lemon
- Sea salt
- Freshly ground black pepper

**SERVES 2**

## Method

Heat the olive oil in a frying pan, add the onion and garlic and cook for 2 minutes. Add the green beans and cook for 3 minutes. Stir in the risotto rice and immediately pour in the stock (broth). Add in the turmeric, peas and lemon juice. Bring it to a boil then reduce to a simmer for around 30 minutes or until all the liquid has been absorbed and the rice is tender. Add hot water if necessary. Add in the nutritional yeast and parsley and stir well. Season with salt and pepper.

# Spinach & Lentil Curry

## Ingredients

125g (4oz) lentils

100g (3½ oz) fresh spinach leaves

3 cloves of garlic, chopped

1 large onion, chopped

1 red chilli, finely chopped

1 carrot, chopped

1 tablespoon tomato purée (tomato paste)

2 teaspoons curry powder

200mls (7fl oz) coconut milk

360mls (12fl oz) vegetable stock (broth)

1 teaspoon olive oil or coconut oil

1 large handful of fresh coriander (cilantro), chopped

**SERVES 2**

## Method

Heat the oil in a frying pan and add the carrot and onion and cook for 5 minutes. Add the chilli and garlic and cook for 1 minute. Stir in the lentils, tomato puree (paste), curry powder and coconut milk. Stir well. Add in the stock (broth). Bring it to a boil, cover and simmer for 20 minutes. Add in the spinach and cook for around 3 minutes until the spinach has wilted. Sprinkle in the coriander (cilantro) and enjoy.

# Baked Pumpkin & Red Onion Lentils

## Ingredients

225g (8oz) lentils

2 red onions, quartered

1 small pumpkin, deseed and cut into slices

2 tomatoes, diced

3 whole cloves of garlic

1 teaspoon chilli powder

1 teaspoon ground ginger

2 teaspoons cumin

1 litre (1½ pints) vegetable stock (broth)

3 tablespoons olive oil

1 small handful of fresh parsley or coriander (cilantro)

Sea salt

Freshly ground black pepper

**SERVES 4**

## Method

Pour a tablespoon of olive oil into a roasting tin and lay the pumpkin slices into it. Transfer it to the oven and bake at 180C/360F for around 25 minutes. In the meantime, heat 2 tablespoons of olive oil in a large frying pan. Add in the red onions and garlic and cook for 2 minutes. Add in the tomatoes, chilli, ginger and cumin and cook for 1 minute. Add in the lentils and pour in the stock (broth). Stir well. Season with salt and pepper. Bring it to the boil, reduce the heat and simmer for around 20 minutes or until the lentils are tender. Serve the pumpkin slices on top of the lentils and sprinkle with parsley or coriander (cilantro).

# VEGAN DESSERTS & SNACKS

# Pineapple Cream Cake

## Ingredients

FOR THE BASE:

225g (8oz) ground almonds (almond flour/almond meal)

3 tablespoons coconut oil

2 tablespoons water

Pinch of salt

FOR THE FILLING:

450g (1lb) tinned crushed pineapple, drained

2 teaspoons icing sugar

400mls (14fl oz) coconut milk

Pinch of salt

SERVES
8

## Method

Place the ground almonds (almond flour/almond meal), coconut oil, water and salt into a bowl and combine them. Press the almond mixture into a spring-form baking tin. Transfer it to the oven and bake at 170C/350F for 15 minutes. Allow it to cool. Pour the coconut milk into a food processor, add the pineapple and sugar and mix them well. Spoon the pineapple mixture on top of the cool base. Cover it and chill it in the fridge before serving.

# Plum & Apple Crumble

## Ingredients

25g (1oz) brown sugar
5 apples, peeled, cored and sliced
5 plums, stones removed and quartered
1/2 teaspoon cinnamon
50mls (2fl oz) apple juice

FOR THE CRUMBLE:
175g (7oz) oats
75g (3oz) coconut oil
50g (2oz) brown sugar
1/2 teaspoon cinnamon

**SERVES 4**

## Method

Preheat the oven to 180C/360F. Scatter the plums, apples, apple juice and cinnamon in an ovenproof pie dish. In a bowl, mix together the oats, coconut oil, brown sugar and cinnamon. Scoop the oat mixture over the fruit. Transfer it to the oven and bake for 30 minutes.

# Chocolate Protein Cashew Bars

**MAKES 12**

## Ingredients

125g (4oz) pitted dates

150g (5oz) unsalted cashews

50g (2oz) 100% vegan cocoa powder or cacao nibs

1 scoop vegan protein powder

3 tablespoons almond milk

Pinch of salt

## Method

Place all of the ingredients into a food processor and process until everything is well combined. Transfer the mixture to a small baking tin and smooth it out. Cover it and place it in the fridge for at least an hour before cutting it into bars.

# Nut & Pumpkin Protein Bars

## Ingredients

125g (4oz) almonds, roughly chopped

100g (3½ oz) peanut butter

75g (3oz) sunflower seeds

75g (3oz) pumpkin seeds

50g (2oz) Brazil nuts, chopped

50g (2oz) oats

25g (1oz) raisins

1 banana, peeled and mashed

1 teaspoon ground cinnamon

3 tablespoons maple syrup

Pinch of sea salt

**MAKES 16**

## Method

Place the maple syrup and peanut butter into a saucepan and gently warm it until it melts, then remove it from the heat. Place the oats, pumpkin seeds, almonds, sunflower seeds, Brazil nuts, raisins, cinnamon and salt into a bowl and mix well. Stir the peanut butter mixture and mashed banana into the nuts and seeds. Preheat the oven to 180C/360F. Grease and line a square baking tin with parchment paper. Scoop the mixture into the tin, pressing it into the edges. Transfer it to the oven and bake at 180C/360F for 15-20 minutes. Allow them to cool before cutting into bars. Enjoy.

# Baked Passion Fruit Plums

## Ingredients

450g (1lb) plums, halved and stones removed
4 passion fruits, halved
1 teaspoon cinnamon

**SERVES 4-6**

## Method

Preheat the oven to 180C/360F. Place the plums into an ovenproof dish with the cut side facing up. Sprinkle the plums with cinnamon. Transfer them to the oven and bake for 25 minutes. Spoon the passion fruit seeds over the plums and return them to the oven to warm them. Serve with soya cream.

# Vegan Sticky Toffee Pudding

## Ingredients

175g (6oz) pitted dates, chopped

100g (3½ oz) brown sugar

100g (3½ oz) apple puree or apple sauce

175g (6oz) plain flour

1 teaspoon baking soda

1 teaspoon baking powder

1 teaspoon vanilla extract

100mls (3½ fl oz) almond milk

150mls (5fl oz) boiling water

75mls (3fl oz) olive oil

FOR THE TOFFEE SAUCE:

100g (3½ oz) brown sugar

125mls (4fl oz) coconut milk

Pinch of salt

## Method

Place the dates in a large bowl. Pour the boiling water into the bowl and add the baking soda and vanilla extract. Mash the mixture well. Preheat the oven to 180C/360F. Grease 6 ramekin dishes with oil and line them with grease-proof paper. In a separate bowl, combine the olive oil and brown sugar. Add in the apple, almond milk and dates mixture. Add in the baking powder and flour and mix thoroughly. Spoon the mixture into the ramekins to around 2/3 full. Transfer them to the oven and cook for 35-40 minutes or until firm. Remove and allow them to cool.

FOR THE TOFFEE SAUCE: Sprinkle the sugar into a saucepan and place it on a low heat and warm it until it has completely melted then remove it from the heat. Warm the coconut milk separately. Slowly add the coconut milk, stirring constantly to prevent lumps. You can return it to the heat whilst stirring to dissolve any lumps. Add a pinch of salt. Serve the sponges and pour the toffee sauce over the top. Eat straight away.

# Coconut & Nut Butter Truffles

**MAKES approx. 24**

## Ingredients

125g (4oz) almond butter

75g (3oz) desiccated (shredded) coconut

75g (3oz) chopped almonds

2 tablespoons tahini paste

2 teaspoons maple syrup (or to taste)

Extra coconut for rolling

## Method

Place the coconut, tahini, almond butter and chopped almonds into a bowl and combine them thoroughly. Stir in a maple syrup then taste to check the sweetness. Add a little more syrup if you need to. Roll the mixture into balls. Scatter some desiccated (shredded) coconut on a plate and coat the balls in it. Keep them refrigerated until ready to use.

# Cookie Dough Bars

## Ingredients

MAKES
9

100g (3½ oz) oats

75g (3oz) almond butter

2 teaspoons vanilla extract

2 teaspoons maple syrup

150mls (5fl oz) almond milk

## Method

Place the oats into a food processor and process until powdery. Add in the almond butter, syrup and vanilla extract. Slowly add in the almond milk until it becomes doughy. Grease and line a small baking tin. Spoon the dough mixture into the tin and smooth it out. Cover and place it in the fridge for at least 3 hours. Cut the mixture into bars. Keep refrigerated.

# VEGAN DIPS, SAUCES & DRESSINGS

# Creamy Maple Dressing

## Ingredients

1 tablespoon maple syrup
1 tablespoon tahini paste
2 tablespoons olive oil
1 tablespoon apple cider vinegar

**SERVES 2**

## Method

Combine all of the ingredients in a bowl and season with pepper.

# Thyme & Lemon Oil Dressing

## Ingredients

1 clove of garlic
1 teaspoon maple syrup
Juice of 1 lemon
4 tablespoons olive oil
Small bunch of thyme

**SERVES 2**

## Method

Place all the ingredients into a blender and blitz until smooth.

# Coriander & Lime Dressing

## Ingredients

Juice of 2 limes

1 tablespoon apple cider vinegar

2 tablespoons olive oil

1 small handful of fresh coriander (cilantro), finely chopped

## Method

Place all of the ingredients into a bowl and mix well. Serve it with rice dishes, beans and salads.

# Vinaigrette

## Ingredients

4 tablespoons olive oil

1 tablespoon apple cider vinegar

1/2 teaspoon sea salt

A squeeze of lemon juice

Freshly ground black pepper

## Method

Place all of the ingredients into a bowl or jar and mix well. You can add a clove of garlic, fresh or dried herbs, and a teaspoon of mustard or balsamic to this basic mixture for extra flavour.

# Creamy Orange Dressing

## Ingredients

1 avocado, stone removed and peeled
1 tablespoon tahini
120mls (4fl oz) orange juice
2 tablespoons avocado oil
2 teaspoons soy sauce
Pinch of cayenne pepper

## Method

Place all of the ingredients into a blender and blitz until smooth and creamy. If the dressing seems too thick you can add a little extra juice or oil.

# Balsamic Dressing

## Ingredients

2 tablespoons lemon juice
2 tablespoons balsamic vinegar
1 teaspoon mustard
1 teaspoon dried mixed herbs
1 garlic clove, crushed

SERVES
2

## Method

Place all the ingredients together in a bowl and mix well. This is a really versatile dressing that goes well with a broad range of dishes.

# Peanut & Ginger Dressing

## Ingredients

1 tablespoon peanut butter

1 clove of garlic, peeled and chopped

1 tablespoon olive oil

1/2 teaspoon ground ginger

## Method

Place all the ingredients into a bowl and mix well.

# Smoky Tomato Salsa

## Ingredients

450g (1lb) ripe tomatoes, deseeded and chopped

2 cloves of garlic, peeled and finely chopped

2 tablespoons red wine vinegar

2 tablespoons olive oil

1/2 teaspoon smoked paprika

1/2 teaspoon salt

## Method

Place all of the ingredients into a bowl and mix well. Serve with salads, bean dishes, tacos and tortillas.

# Vegan Pesto

## Ingredients

75g (3oz) pumpkin seeds
3 cloves of garlic
3 tablespoons nutritious yeast
1 large handful of fresh basil
125mls (4fl oz) olive oil

**SERVES 2**

## Method

Place the pumpkin seeds, garlic, yeast and basil into a blender and process until smooth. Add a tablespoon of oil at a time and continue blending until smooth. Serve with tofu and pasta dishes.

# Barbecue Sauce

## Ingredients

150g (5oz) tomato purée (paste)
2 tablespoons mustard
2 tablespoons smoked paprika
1 tablespoon garlic powder
1 teaspoon sea salt
2 teaspoons black pepper
150mls (5fl oz) apple cider vinegar
3-4 tablespoons maple syrup

## Method

Combine all of the ingredients until mixed well. Can be used hot or cold. Use it as a marinade for tofu and vegetables or warm the sauce over a medium heat and serve it with chips, sweet potato fries or burgers.

# Guacamole

## Ingredients

12 ripe avocados

1 clove garlic

1 red chilli pepper, finely chopped

Juice of ½ lime

**SERVES 2-4**

## Method

Remove the stone from the avocados and scoop out the flesh. Place all the ingredients in a bowl and mash together until smooth or alternatively use a food processor. Serve with crackers, toast, loaded potatoes, with raw crudités or as a sandwich filler.

# Beetroot Hummus

## Ingredients

400g (14oz) tin of chickpeas, drained and rinsed

225g (8oz) cooked beetroot

Pinch of salt

Juice of ½ lemon

2 cloves of garlic, peeled

2 tablespoons tahini

1 teaspoon ground cumin

100mls (3½ fl oz) olive oil

## Method

Place all of the ingredients into a blender and blitz until smooth. Serve as a dip or in Buddha bowls and salads.

# Hummus

## Ingredients

400g (14oz) tin of chickpeas (garbanzo beans), drained and rinsed

2 cloves of garlic, peeled

1 tablespoon olive oil

Juice of 1 lemon

1 teaspoon sea salt

Extra oil for garnish

## Method

Place all the ingredients in a food processor and mix until smooth and creamy. Spoon it into a bowl and add a little swirl of olive oil on top.

You may also be interested in other titles by
**Erin Rose Publishing**
which are available in both paperback and ebook.

**Quick Start Guides**

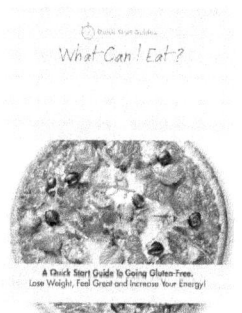

What Can I Eat?
**SUGAR FREE DIET**
A Quick Start Guide To Quitting Sugar.
Lose Weight, Feel Great and Increase Your Energy!

The Essential
**SUGAR FREE DIET**
COOKBOOK
A Quick Start Guide To Sugar Free Cooking.
Over 100 New and Delicious Sugar Free Recipes!

The Essential
**SUGAR FREE FAMILY**
COOKBOOK
A Quick Start Guide To
Helping Your Family Quit Sugar.
Plus Over 100 Healthy And Delicious Family-Friendly Recipes

The Essential
**SUGAR FREE DESSERTS**
RECIPE BOOK
A Quick Start Guide To Cooking Sugar-Free Cakes,
Desserts and Sweet Treats
Over 70 Heavenly And Delicious Sugar-Free Recipes
To Make Quitting Sugar Easy

The Essential
**SUGAR FREE SLOW COOKER**
Recipe Book
A Quick Start Guide To Healthy Sugar Free Slow Cooking.
90 Simple And Delicious Calorie Counted
Recipes For Weight Loss and Good Health.

The Essential
**SUGAR FREE DIET**
Meals For One
A Quick Start Guide To Cooking Sugar Free Meals For One.
Simple And Delicious Calorie Counted Recipes For One. Never
Lose Weight And Improve Your Health.

The Essential
**BLOOD SUGAR DIET**
RECIPE BOOK
A Quick Start Guide To Cooking On The Blood Sugar Diet
Lose Weight And Transforming Your Body
PLUS Over 80 Delicious Low Carb Recipes

The New Essential
**BLOOD SUGAR DIET**
COOKBOOK
A Quick Start Guide To Balancing Your Blood Sugar Through Diet.
Improve Your Health And Lose Weight

Family Favourites
A Quick Start Guide To Help Your Family Get Healthier

The Essential
**BLOOD SUGAR DIET**
15 Minute Meals
A Quick Start Guide To Cooking Quick Easy Meals
On The Blood Sugar Diet
Over 85 Calorie Counted Recipes To Lose Weight
And Transform Your Body

The Essential
**BLOOD SUGAR DIET**
MEALS FOR ONE
A Quick Start Guide To Cooking On The Blood Sugar Diet
Over 80 Easy And Delicious Calorie Counted Recipes For One

Recipes For Life
A Quick Start Guide To The Blood Sugar Diet

The
**LOW CARB HIGH FAT**
DIET
A Quick Start Guide To The Low Carb High Fat Diet
Lose Weight And Feel Great.
PLUS over 100 Delicious Low Carb Recipes For Weight Loss

The Essential
**LOW CARB HIGH FAT DIET**
COOKBOOK
A Quick Start Guide To Cooking Low Carb High Fat Cooking
Over 120 New and Delicious Low Carb High Fat
Recipes For Weight Loss

The Essential
**LOW CARB DIET MEALS**
FOR ONE
A Quick Start Guide To Cooking Low Carb Meals For One

What Can I Eat?
A Quick Start Guide To Going Gluten-Free.
Lose Weight, Feel Great and Increase Your Energy!

## HEALTHY GUT DIET RECIPE BOOK

*The Essential*

A Quick Start Guide To Improving Your Digestion, Health And Wellbeing
PLUS over 90 Delicious Gut-Friendly Recipes

## Low FODMAP Diet COOKBOOK

*The Essential*

A Quick Start Guide To Relieving the Symptoms of IBS Through Diet
Improve Your Digestion, Health And Wellbeing
PLUS over 75 IBS-Friendly Recipes!

## DIABETES DIET COOKBOOK

*the Essential*

A Quick Start Guide To Managing Your Diabetes Through Diet

## ALKALINE DIET SOLUTION

*the*

A Quick Start Guide To The Alkaline Diet
Lose Weight, Improve Your Health and Feel Great!
PLUS over 90 Alkaline-Friendly Recipes

## THYROID DIET RECIPE BOOK

*The Essential*

A Quick Start Guide To Healing Your Thyroid Through Diet. Lose Weight And Feel Great - With Delicious Thyroid-Friendly Recipes

## SIRT FOOD DIET RECIPE BOOK

*The Essential*

A Quick Start Guide to Cooking on the SIRT Food Diet
Over 100 Easy and Delicious Recipes to Help You Lose Weight & Feel Great on a Sirt Food Diet

## DAIRY FREE DIET

*What Can I Eat?* ON A

A Quick Start Guide To Quitting Dairy and Lactose
Lose Weight, Feel Great and Increase Your Energy!
PLUS 100 Delicious Dairy-Free Recipes

## LOWER CHOLESTEROL DIET

A Quick Start Guide To Lower Cholesterol

## THE VEGAN 15 MINUTE COOKBOOK

Over 100 Simple And Delicious Vegan Recipes For Everyone

## ROASTING TIN COOKBOOK

*The Essential*

Over 80 Easy And Delicious One Dish, No-Fuss Oven Recipes

## Blood Sugar Diet Diary

## Diabetes Diet Diary

## My Diet Diary

Daily Diet, Health And Fitness Diary To Track Weight Loss And Well-being

## Low FODMAP Food Diary

## Sugar-Free Diet Diary

Daily Diary For Cutting Sugar, Losing Weight and Feeling Great

## FOOD Diary

# Books by Sophie Ryan
## Erin Rose Publishing

**energy balls**
Sophie Ryan

30 Simple And Delicious Superfood Energy Balls And Bites
Recipes For Great Health and Wellbeing

**energy bars**
Sophie Ryan

Over 30 Easy And Delicious Superfood Energy Bars
Recipes To Boost Your Vitality

Sophie Ryan

30 Simple And Tasty Energy Shots And Smoothies
To Power Up Your Health And Well-Being

www.ingramcontent.com/pod-product-compliance
Lightning Source LLC
Chambersburg PA
CBHW081257040426
42452CB00014B/2535